This is one of a series of books on modern art help very young people learn the basic vocabulary used by artists, a sort of ABC of art. Parents and teachers play a key role in this learning process, encouraging careful, thoughtful looking. This book isolates storytelling aspects of works of art to show how they are used by artists and how they contribute to meaning in art. By looking for stories and discussing what ideas and feelings they suggest, adults encourage children to develop creative thinking skills. At the back of this book, there is more information about the pictures included to help in this engaging process.

Enjoy looking together!

Stories

Philip Yenawine

The Museum of Modern Art, New York
Delacorte Press

Acknowledgements
This book was made possible by the generosity of The Eugene and
Estelle Ferkauf Foundation; John and Margot Ernst; David Rockefeller,
Jr.; John and Jodie Eastman; Joan Ganz Cooney; and The Astrid
Johansen Memorial Gift Fund. Of equal importance were the talents of
Takaaki Matsumoto, Michael McGinn, Mikio Sakai, David Gale, Harriet
Bee, Richard Tooke, Mikki Carpenter, Nancy Miller, Alexander Gray,
Carlos Silveira, and particularly Catherine Grimshaw. I am extremely
grateful to all of them.

Library of Congress Cataloging in Publication Data

Yenawine, Philip.
Stories/by Philip Yenawine.
         p   cm.
Summary: Isolates the artistic element of story, what is happening in a
painting, and discusses how story contributes to a work of art through
examples from The Museum of Modern Art in New York.
ISBN 0-385-30256-8 (trade). –ISBN 0-385-30316-5 (lib. ed.)
[1. Art appreciation.]   I. Title.
N7477.Y46 1991
701'.1–dc20   90-38986   CIP   AC
ISBN 0-87070-178-9 (MoMA)

Cover: Jacob Lawrence. *The Migration of the Negro*. 1940–41. 12 x 18"
(30.5 x 45.7 cm). The Museum of Modern Art, New York. Gift of Mrs.
David M. Levy.

The Museum of Modern Art
11 West 53 Street
New York, NY 10019

Delacorte Press
Bantam Doubleday Dell Publishing Group, Inc.
666 Fifth Avenue
New York, New York 10103

Printed in Italy

In pictures, you can make up stories about people . . . and places . . . and things.

Details from (clockwise from upper left) Marc Chagall, *Birthday* (p. 19); Henri Matisse, *Piano Lesson* (p. 17); Salvador Dali, *The Persistence of Memory* (p. 5); Andrew Wyeth, *Christina's World* (p. 15)

Sometimes the stories are a little like whispering secrets.

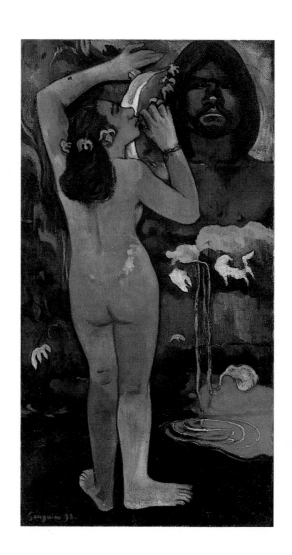

Paul Gauguin, *The Moon and the Earth*

And they can be mysterious.

Odilon Redon, *Silence*

They can play tricks. Is it daytime in this picture, or is it night?

René Magritte, *The Empire of Light, II*

Can you tell the time on these pocket watches? What else is strange about this picture?

Salvador Dali, *The Persistence of Memory*

Maybe it's time to eat. What meal is this? How can you tell?

Pierre Bonnard, *The Breakfast Room*

Some paintings and sculptures show families being together.
What can you tell about this family?

Henry Moore, *Family Group*

Can you tell more about these parents and children? Pretend you know them.

Marisol (Marisol Escobar), *The Family;* Dorothea Lange, *First Born, Berkeley*

You have to use your imagination to figure out who is the mother, father, and child in this family.

Joan Miró, *The Family*, plate IV from *Series I*

You can also

make pictures

of the city —

full of buildings,

cars, and signs.

Look at the

colors and lines.

Can you hear

any noise?

Jean Dubuffet, *Business Prospers*

Here's an old-fashioned movie theater. What do you think the young woman is thinking?

Edward Hopper, *New York Movie*

How is this man feeling? What do you think he is looking at?

Marc Chagall, *Self-Portrait with Grimace*

How many differences can you find between this woman . . .

Roy Lichtenstein, *Girl with Ball*

and this one? Make up a story about what they are doing. How do you think they feel?

Andrew Wyeth, *Christina's World*

What are these three girls doing?
Where do you think they are?

Jacob Lawrence, *The Migration of the Negro*

Do you think this boy wants to practice the piano? Where do you think he would like to be instead?

Henri Matisse, *Piano Lesson*

**These girls are swinging from a pole.
Does it seem dangerous?
What about the building behind them?**

Ben Shahn, *Liberation*

Look at these two people. Where are they? What are they doing?

Marc Chagall, *Birthday*

**Pictures are almost like dreams.
Here is someone sleeping on a patchwork
quilt. Does she look comfortable?**

Romare Bearden, *Patchwork Quilt*

Maybe she is dreaming of a quiet night and a gentle lion. What else can you imagine about this story?

Henri Rousseau, *The Sleeping Gypsy*

Do you have any secrets or mysteries to draw? Any funny stories to tell in pictures?

The art in this book can be found at The Museum of Modern Art in New York City. Other museums and galleries have many interesting pictures too, and it is good to make a habit of visiting them, looking for stories. You can also look in magazines, books, buildings, parks, and gardens.

Page 2

Paul Gauguin
The Moon and the Earth, 1893
Oil on burlap
45 x 24 1/2" (11.4 x 62.2 cm)
Lillie P. Bliss Collection

Finding in Tahiti an essence he felt missing in his native France, Gauguin often drew the local people and terrain of his adopted home, creating his own myths and archetypes.

Page 3

Odilon Redon
Silence, c. 1911
Oil on gesso on paper
21 1/4 x 21 1/2" (54 x 54.6 cm)
Lillie P. Bliss collection

Trying to probe essential mysteries, Redon often created cryptic scenes such as this, representing silence with a symbolic gesture, downcast eyes, deep shadows, and spiraling lines.

Page 4

René Magritte
The Empire of Light, II, 1950
Oil on canvas
31 x 39" (78.8 x 99.1 cm)
Gift of D. and J. de Menil

Magritte's form of Surrealism (going beyond what we perceive to be real) involved depicting recognizable phenomena in impossible relationships.

Page 5

Salvador Dali
The Persistence of Memory, 1931
Oil on canvas
9 1/2 x 13" (24.1 x 33 cm)
Given anonymously

Dali, another Surrealist, went further in imagination than Magritte, incorporating real and distorted elements to create disjointed, dreamlike images.

Page 6

Pierre Bonnard
The Breakfast Room, c. 1930–31
Oil on canvas
62 7/8 x 44 7/8" (159.6 x 113.8 cm)
Given anonymously

Bonnard's work depicts domesticity through beautiful colors, warm light, and sketchy brushwork that seems to be forever fresh, if slightly distorted.

Page 7

Henry Moore
Family Group, 1948–49
Bronze (cast 1950)
59 1/4 x 46 1/2 x 29 7/8" (150.5 x 118 x 75.9 cm) including base
A. Conger Goodyear Fund

In Moore's sculpture a pattern of interlocking forms and rhythmic contours help symbolize family unity and harmony.

Page 8

Marisol (Marisol Escobar)
The Family, 1962
Printed wood and other materials in
three sections
Overall 6' 10 5/8" x 65 1/2" x 15 1/2"
(209.8 x 166.3 x 39.3 cm)
Advisory Committee Fund

Marisol's fatherless group has the
spare, straightforward simplicity
of Depression-era photographs,
a family perhaps impoverished but
not poor.

Page 8

Dorothea Lange
First Born, Berkeley, 1952
Gelatin-silver print
19 3/8 x 15 1/2" (49.2 x 39.5 cm)
Purchase

Direct and honest, Lange used no
artifice to picture the unsentimental
but still tender bond between a
father and infant.

Page 9

Joan Miró
The Family, plate IV from *Series I,*
1952
Etching, engraving, and aquatint,
printed in color
14 15/16 x 17 7/8" (38 x 45.4 cm)
Curt Valentin Bequest

Miró often adopted methods that
seem childlike in his attempt to cut
through acquired knowledge to
more basic understandings of things.

Page 11

Jean Dubuffet
Business Prospers, from the Paris
Circus series, 1961
Oil on canvas
65" x 7' 2 5/8" (165.5 x 220 cm)
Mrs. Simon Guggenheim Fund

Both intrigued and put off by the
force of modern life, Dubuffet
employed a very edgy line and
strong colors in his cartoonlike,
slightly macabre representations of
people and places.

Page 12

Edward Hopper
New York Movie, 1939
Oil on canvas
32 1/4 x 40 1/8" (81.9 x 101.9 cm)
Given anonymously

Hopper's paintings employ rich
colors that seem to glow with light
and also clearly evoke a mood full
of associations and memories.

Page 13

Marc Chagall
Self-Portrait with Grimace, 1924–25
Etching and aquatint
14 11/16 x 10 3/4" (37 x 27.3 cm)
Gift of the artist

Appealingly unglamorous, Chagall
presents himself as a wide-eyed
energetic man, his character
enhanced by the distorted mouth.

Page 14

Roy Lichtenstein
Girl with Ball, 1961
Oil and synthetic polymer paint
on canvas
60 1/4 x 36 1/4" (153 x 91.9 cm)
Gift of Philip Johnson

Both amused and inspired by
cartoon imagery, Lichtenstein
capitalizes on stylized and stereo-
typic simplifications that become
signs and emblems, rather than
accurate descriptions of arms,
waves, and tossed hair.

Page 15

Andrew Wyeth
Christina's World, 1948
Tempera on gesso panel
32 1/4 x 47 3/4" (81.9 x 121.3 cm)
Purchase

This woman's back is turned to us.
We are unable to see her expression,
yet easily able to picture ourselves in
her place. Our empathy perhaps
explains the painting's enormous
appeal.